In Our Backyards: Public and Private Gardens of the Texas Coastal Bend

Published by the Corpus Christi Botanical Gardens & Nature Center

CONTENTS

DEDICATION

This book is dedicated to all gardeners who tirelessly work clay, caliche and sand to make the Texas Coastal Bend bloom.

In Our Backyards: Public and Private Gardens of the Texas Coastal Bend published by the Botanical and Nature Institute of South Texas, Inc. d.b.a. the Corpus Christi Botanical Gardens & Nature Center.

ISBN 0-9766235-0-1

Produced by John C. Watson, Jr.

Photo editor: John Watson

Content editor: Carole Peterson

Copy editors: MaryJane Crull, Michael Womack

Contributing writers: MaryJane Crull, Deanna Payne, Carole Peterson, John Watson, Michael Womack

Location coordinator: Deanna Payne

Plant identification: Sam Jones, Paul Thorton, Michael Womack

Book design: Martell Speigner and John Watson

Printed in U.S.A. by Grunwald Printing, Inc., Corpus Christi, Texas

Distributed by Texas A&M University Press, College Station, Texas

Sinton Garden Club Butterfly Garden

A Zebra Long Wing visits a garden created by Kingsville Master Gardeners.

Children's Discovery Garden in Rockport

In Our Backyards

Public and Private Gardens of the Texas Coastal Bend

CONTENTS

◄ Kingsville Master Gardeners received state recognition for creating a wildlife habitat garden project using Xeriscape principles, native plants, and English garden design.

FOREWORD

Gardening is an intensive labor of love. It is a love born of different reasons. For some of us, it is a way to release pent-up creative energies; for others, an inquiry into the nature of nature; for still others, it is a way to totally relax and leave the real world in the garden shed while we bring out the tools. Regardless of the reason, the results are the same: beautiful and interesting spaces that are—as much as a Monet water lily painting—the personal expressions of their creators.

This book is a labor of love as well. Deanna Payne took on the difficult task of getting photographers and gardeners together in the same place at the same time. Barbra Riley, my photography instructor at Texas A&M University-Corpus Christi, provided many reality checks and much encouragement when winters were dark and spring was far away. Carole Peterson, a sensitive writer and a critical editor, wove together the stories you will read among the pictures. Martell Speigner at Grunwald Printing has worked tirelessly around our erratic schedules to perfect the design of the book. The Board of Directors of the Corpus Christi Botanical Gardens & Nature Center, especially Presidents Dr. Michael Womack and Betty Whitt, deserve so much credit for getting behind this project early on. Thanks to all of you for believing!

Of course, the book would not exist without the efforts of the gardeners, most of whom were nominated by their peers in the many garden clubs and plant societies that appear in this book. Special thanks to our early supporters, Helen Orsak and the Nueces County Master Gardeners, Dixie Oshman and the Ocean Drive Garden Club, and Jan Shannon and the Corpus Christi Rose Society.

Finally, we all owe a tremendous debt of gratitude for the long-suffering patience of my wife and fellow Master Gardener, Kay, who endured years of afternoons and weekends when I would come in from work and take off to photograph gardens or edit photos on the computer. For a while, anyway, we have our life back!

John C. Watson, Jr.

Summer, 2005

INTRODUCTION

Have you ever wondered what lay behind the walls and gates that enclose many of the yards of South Texas? Those tall fences where trailing vines and towering treetops contrast with the suburban sameness of neighboring lawns? *In Our Backyards: Public and Private Gardens of the Texas Coastal Bend* is the first book to take readers behind the walls and fences to celebrate some of the most interesting and beautiful garden spots in South Texas. From the Live Oak Peninsula to the shores of Baffin Bay, from the dunes of the barrier islands to the limestone hills of the deep brush country, we are treated to a tour of gardens public and private, tiny and stately, manicured and wild, all of which, no matter what the size or style, reflect the gardener's love for the natural beauty of the Texas Coastal Bend.

Gardeners from Rockport to Kingsville, and Port Aransas to Alice have opened their gates and welcomed photographer John Watson and his associates to their gardens to give visitors a rare glimpse of these hidden horticultural treasures. Both novice and experienced gardeners will enjoy this photographic tour of the hidden beauty found "In Our Backyards."

Carole L. Peterson   Summer, 2005

◀ Front of Dr. Alvaro and Carmen Ramos's Ocean Drive home

THE TEXAS COASTAL BEND

The Texas Coastal Bend is defined by its gentle southward curve around the northwestern corner of the Gulf of Mexico, extending from San Antonio Bay to the southern reaches of the upper Laguna Madre. Along the shoreline, long, low islands form sandy barriers across the mouths of coastal bays and estuaries. On shore, a broad alluvial plain bisected by the Nueces River fans northwestward to a limestone slope that marks the end of the Central Great Plains. It is here in South Texas that coastal plains gently overlap the arid thorn shrub region of the Tamaulipan Biotic Province, and the history of Mexico and the United States merge.

History

Early explorers described the Texas Coastal Bend as marshlands and treeless grassland prairie teeming with wildlife. Alonzo Alvarez de Piñeda mapped its shoreline in 1519, claiming the region for the King of Spain. Navigating the shallow bays proved treacherous for those who followed, and the overland journey from Mexico across blistering desert even more so. Despite several attempts, there were few European settlements in the area. For another two centuries the land remained pristine, inhabited primarily by Karankawas, Comanches and Lipan Apaches who roamed the coastal prairies following game and harvesting seasonal plants such as cactus fruit, pecans and berries.

In 1746, the vast coastal area from Tampico to the San Antonio River was designated the State of Nuevo Santender. Inducements to settle the arid brushland north of the Rio Grande River attracted Spanish ranchers who saw opportunity in the wild herds of mustangs and longhorn cattle that roamed there. The Spaniards' enormous, isolated ranches were forerunners of the cattle kingdoms that have come to symbolize life in Texas.

In 1821, Mexico gained independence from Spain and the land south of the Nueces River became part of the State of Tamaulipas. The following year, Stephen F. Austin and a growing number of English, Irish, Czech and German immigrants began settling in central Texas. By 1835, the Texians, as they were called, rebelled against the Mexican dictatorship of General Antonio López de Santa Ana and formed the Republic of Texas. After the revolution, it remained unclear whether the border separating Mexico and Texas was the Nueces or the Rio Grande River, and Mexico continued issuing land grants in the disputed area.

Texas was annexed by the United States in 1845. Three years later its border along the Rio Grande River was firmly established by the Treaty of Guadalupe-Hidalgo. In the treaty, the United States recognized the validity of all land grants made by Spain or Mexico up until 1848.

One such grant was to adventurer and impresario Colonel Henry Lawrence Kinney, who in 1840 had purchased a portion of a Mexican grant to establish a trading post at the mouth of the Nueces River on Corpus Christi Bay. Located at the center of the Texas Coastal Bend, Kinney promoted the area as "Naples on the Gulf" to attract settlers. By 1850, the town's population had reached 689 inhabitants and the name "Corpus Christi" had emerged.

In 1852, riverboat captain Richard King made a trip on horseback from Brownsville to Kinney's growing settlement. King was impressed with the potential

◄ Sunset over Bird Island

of the vast lands south of Corpus Christi, known as the Wild Horse Desert, and purchased a large Mexican land grant near Baffin Bay. Relying on the time-tested expertise of the Mexican *vaqueros*, King and his family transformed South Texas ranching from a subsistence lifestyle to a diversified cattle industry. By 1885, King had amassed 614,000 acres. Today, the King Ranch covers 825,000 acres of South Texas ranchland.

Thirty miles northeast of Corpus Christi on a peninsula between Copano and Aransas Bays, the town of Rockport was founded as a seaport to ship cattle, hides and tallow after the Civil War. In the neighboring town of Fulton, an ornate four-story house was constructed for cattleman George W. Fulton at a cost of $100,000. Completed in 1876, the structure was a technological marvel with innovations such as central ventilation, forced air heating, and hot and cold running water.

By the 1880s, Rockport-Fulton began to blossom as a tourist resort with visitors arriving by train to enjoy the sea, sand, and sun. As early as 1907, Rockport residents took a lead in conservation efforts to protect game, fish, and wildlife. In 1937, the Aransas Migratory Waterfowl Refuge was established on Blackjack Peninsula, near Rockport. Today the Aransas National Wildlife Refuge comprises 54,829 acres of scattered blackjack oak woodlands, fresh and saltwater marshes, ponds, and coastal grasslands on the mainland, as well as 56,668 acres on Matagorda Island. It is the winter home of the endangered whooping crane.

In 1889, promoter Colonel Elihu Ropes arrived in the Coastal Bend from New Jersey. Attracted by the climate and proximity to the Gulf of Mexico, Ropes launched several ambitious enterprises. One was the Port of Ropesville on Mustang Island. Rope's plans for a deepwater port failed, but the town flourished as a resort and fishing community. In 1896, its name was changed to Tarpon to celebrate the local fishing. In 1911, the name Port Aransas was adopted. Today, the coastal community continues to attract thousands of visitors each year to enjoy its miles of public beach for fishing, swimming, and birding.

The historic Fulton Mansion was a technological marvel in 1876.

Herb garden at Fulton Mansion

White pelicans and other coastal birds roost on a Rockport pier.

Environment

The Texas Coastal Bend is a biological crossroads where humid coastal prairies and marshes intersect arid brushlands and coastal estuary ecosystems. Subtle transitions from north to south and east to west support the greatest diversity of flora and fauna in Texas. South Texas lies at the convergence of primary migration routes for North American butterflies, birds, and mammals. Here are found both tropical species venturing northward and colder climate species moving southward.

The landscape has changed dramatically from the days of vast grassland prairies interrupted only by occasional rivers lined with mesquite, live oak, and pecan trees or thickets of spiny thorn brush. Cattle drives, suppression of natural wildfires, and loss of the great migratory bison herds altered the balance of nature. Also, pioneers did not anticipate the adaptability and invasive nature of some of the plants they

Windswept oaks on Lamar Peninsula

introduced to the semi-tropical climate of the Coastal Bend. As a result, the survival of some native species of flora and fauna is threatened.

Climate is a primary factor in determining which plants will thrive in an area. The Coastal Bend is characterized by long, hot summers, and short mild winters with infrequent freezes. An extended growing season is a benefit many northern gardeners envy. However, the scorching summer sun, months of temperatures soaring near the century mark, and strong prevailing coastal winds present serious challenges. Less than perfect soils are another challenge with significant regional variations ranging from dry, shifting coastal sand, to black gumbo clay and caliche pastureland. Add to that the low annual precipitation that often comes in the form of tropical deluges interspersed with months of drought.

A carpet of bluebonnets at the Rockport Cemetery reminds visitors of the renewal of life.

Public Gardens

Despite the challenges, creative and disciplined gardeners have worked around horticultural perils of the Coastal Bend's growing conditions, and created some of the most interesting and stunning garden spots in Texas. Over the years, the landscape of the Coastal Bend has developed its own distinct character, a blend of Texas heritage and coastal contemporary featuring a mix of native and tropical plants. Municipal parks, churches, museums, and other public venues provide passersby with wonderful opportunities to savor the beauty and unique flavor of the area.

Public gardens also can teach the important role plants play in the natural world. At Rafael Galvan Elementary a butterfly garden was created to provide hands-on learning experiences about plant and animal life cycles.

The Corpus Christi Church of the Good Shepherd is known for its courtyard with oleanders shaped into small specimen trees.

In springtime, the courtyard of the First Presbyterian Church in Corpus Christi is filled with white blossoms of an ornamental pear tree.

Brilliantly colored bougainvillea forms a colorful backdrop for the fountain sculpture, "Blooming Cranes," at Water Street Market in downtown Corpus Christi.

Another fountain cools a plaza ringed by oleanders at Texas A&M University-Corpus Christi.

SOUTH TEXAS BRUSH COUNTRY

Cowboys, cattle, and cactus are images that often come to mind when a non-Texan thinks of the Lone Star State. Little wonder, since it is here in the South Texas Brush Country that the King Ranch, the world's oldest and largest cattle ranch, gave birth to the U.S. ranching industry in the mid-1800s.

Burns Garden

Ranchers Mac and Mary Dru Burns learned to garden with and around conditions of the brush country after literally moving her grandparents' Victorian home from Alice, Texas to their property outside the city limits.

The two-storied Victorian home was built in 1895 and purchased by Mary Dru's grandparents in 1910. Although her family sold it in 1949, she always remembered stories her father told about growing up in the house. Over the years, the house fell into disrepair, until one day while driving by, Mary Dru told Mac, "I wish that house would just burn down. It looks terrible!" Mac had another solution. They purchased the house and moved it north of town. Today it sits on a *caliche* hill overlooking an old-fashioned garden.

Caliche is a layer of soil where the particles are cemented together by lime (calcium carbonate), making it difficult for roots or water to penetrate. In order to create their garden, the Burns had several truckloads of topsoil hauled in to cover the caliche substrate. To keep the topsoil from blowing away, Mary Dru planted

oaks, pomegranates, and weeping bottle brush as wind screens. Finding plants that could tolerate the salt and minerals in the well water was another challenge.

"Some plants would just curl up, and others would manage," she said. "I planted a row of sweet broom that grew for a year and then died off."

Sulfur and Gulf Fritillary butterflies on zinnias. ▶

A butterfly casts a reflection in a mirrored ball. The chrome sphere, an inviting arch and a rustic birdbath are a few of the many surprises hidden in Mary Dru Burns' garden.

Today, her garden is lush and full of bright colored zinnias, lantana, and crepe myrtles. In planning her garden, she followed designs she remembered in her mother's and grandmother's gardens. "I guess that's why mine looks so old-fashioned," she remarked almost apologetically.

"In choosing my plants, I always keep in mind the birds and the butterflies," she said. "My son once told me I was going to have to hand out beekeepers' hats to everyone to keep them from swallowing butterflies!"

Mary Dru does not use any pesticides in the yard so as not to harm the butterflies. Her solution for controlling tomato hornworms that enjoy Mac's vegetable garden is to plant more tomatoes. Whenever they find worms on Mac's tomatoes, they pick them off and put them on Mary Dru's so they can grow into moths.

In addition to the birds, butterflies, and brightly colored flowers, what makes the Burns' garden such a delight for visitors are the surprises hidden around each corner. It may be a piece of statuary, a mirrored ball, a fountain, or a pond. ❧

Gulf Fritillary butterfly

Schubert Garden

When avid gardener, Dr. J.A. Schubert, Sr. of Alice was given an azalea plant by a friend, his emphatic response was, "Azaleas don't grow in this area."

These colorful ornamental shrubs prefer cool, shady locations and moist acidic soil, making them unsuited to the hot, sunny climate and alkaline soils of South Texas. However, after continued pressure from his friend, Dr. Schubert planted the azalea, never expecting it to survive. But it did.

Dr. Schubert began experimenting with other azalea plants. According to his son, Dr. Joseph A. Schubert, Jr., the only ones they could find were marked only as "Azalea." As a result they never knew what they were getting. Some varieties faired well and others did not.

Over the years, the Schuberts learned that *George Tabor* and *Formosa* azaleas grow well in neutral soils. To give them a good start, Dr. Schubert planted them in an acidic soil mixture, mulching them with shredded pine bark each year. He protected the young plants from the heat with a black mesh canopy and daily showers from a hose.

That was more than thirty years ago. Today, the azaleas are well established and large oak trees provide filtered shade. Dr. Schubert, Jr. claims they don't require much more than watering, pruning, and occasional feeding.

The azaleas surrounding Dr. Schubert's home are a local attraction. He uses pine bark mulch to increase the acidity of the soil.

There are times when he thinks of replacing them with something different. But then he receives a letter or a call from someone to say how much they enjoy seeing the azaleas.

"I suppose what I enjoy most about the azaleas is people enjoying them."

So at least for now, Dr. Schubert will continue the tradition his father began. ❧

Harris Garden

A large natural pond creates an oasis of thick, vegetation around Tad and Sheila Harris's home in Kingsville. They purchased the property more than twenty years ago. At that time it was outside the city limits and untouched. When they cleared the center of the property for their home, they kept as many of the native trees and plants as possible. Brush sculpting was used to transition from native landscape to lawn, protecting sensitive areas for wildlife and enhancing areas closer to the house for entertaining and relaxation. When a nearby rail line was abandoned, the Harrises bought the ties to create raised beds, build a fence, and edge walkways. Sheila carefully selected and placed bent ties to create the flowing curve of the front walkway. She created patio areas from large flat rocks and gravel, and did the concrete work herself. She still is adding to her patio and walkway areas to reduce the amount of St. Augustine grass in the yard. ❧

Davis Garden

Visitors to Gary and Sara Davis's home in Kingsville often are surprised by the combination of desert cactus and tropical greenery in the garden.

Gary describes himself as an experimenter. He began his cactus garden with plants given to him by his family, including a rock cactus from his mother that was estimated to be more than two hundred years old.

"I treated that plant better than my first born. Unfortunately the heavy rainfalls over the past year were too much for it, and it finally died."

Gary started his water garden with one small pond. He says he liked the look but not the smell. Then he met a woman who had developed a bog garden with everything planted in pea gravel. Gary tried her technique and found it worked wonderfully.

According to Gary, pea gravel not only reduces smells and mud, it makes it easy to pull up plants to give away – something he always is willing to do. ❧

Gary created a unique fountain by sinking a discarded, eight-foot-long, industrial test tube into a tub of concrete with a waterline running up the middle. He used pea gravel, lava stone, and other decorative rocks to hide the base.

Leubert & Medina Garden

For centuries, South Texas natives and settlers mined cream-colored caliche to make bricks and plaster to build their homes. In the early 1900s, a Kingsville college professor and his family chose to employ ancient methods of forming and stacking caliche bricks to construct their own *Casita de Caliche* (little house of caliche). They followed the traditional *hacienda* design used by the area's early Spanish ranchers who built their main houses around large, interior courtyards to provide safe havens for kitchen gardens, small animals and children.

It was *La Casita de Caliche's* unusual construction and large, central courtyard that drew Dianne Leubert and Roy Medina to purchase the house in 1998. One of the first things Dianne did was to pull large boxwoods out of the courtyard area to provide better views of features like the inlaid painted tile of the Virgin of Guadalupe. The tile is original to the house and symbolizes an important part of Mexican heritage.

According to the legend, a beautiful dark-skinned woman dressed in a blue-green cloak studded with yellow stars appeared to a Catholic Indian, Juan Diego, on a hillside near Mexico City in 1531. Speaking in his native language of Nahuatl, she told him she was the Virgin Mary. She bade him pick roses from a spot where only desert plants could grow and present them to the archbishop as proof of who she was. Juan Diego filled his cloak with the beautiful red roses and did as he was told. When he unfolded the cloak before the archbishop, a likeness of the Virgin appeared upon its folds with the miraculous roses lying at her feet. Over the centuries her image, now known as the Virgin of Guadalupe, has come to symbolize life, hope, and health for people on both sides of the U.S.–Mexican border.

The red climbing rose in the courtyard of *La Casita de Caliche* is one of the plants believed to be original to the house. Other courtyard plants include a large, white crepe myrtle, an antique pink rose, a fig vine, as well as several palms and

Purple trumpet vine

Climbing rose frames view of the Virgin of Guadalupe

ferns. Dianne Leubert also incorporated a number of plants she and Roy brought with them from their previous home including a large *Aloe vera*.

Native to South Texas, *Aloe vera* is a succulent with a wide range of uses from its ornamental beauty to the soothing emollient it produces. Few Coastal Bend homes are without at least one. In the past, these medicinal plants often were passed from one Mexican gardener to another for home cures of burns and cuts.

The focal point of the courtyard is a fountain and pond. Nearby stands a statue of St. Francis of Assisi, patron saint of animals and nature, looking after both real and imaginary creatures that inhabit the garden. The concrete "gator" in the pond came with the house, as did the live gold fish. According to Dianne, the previous owners said the gold fish were there when they purchased the home eighteen years before.

Roy and Dianne work as a team to care for their yard. Dianne is a Master Gardener and does the gardening. Roy takes care of the yard work and watering. They both take pleasure in sitting on the stone bench just outside the kitchen door that opens into the courtyard. There they can relax after a busy day and enjoy the tranquil beauty of their private garden. ❧

A statue of St. Francis protects the animals that inhabit Diane Leubert and Roy Medina's courtyard garden, including a make-believe alligator.

Coastal Prairies & Marshes

Traveling towards the coast from Kingsville, brush country gives way to coastal prairie and marshes. At one time, more than nine million acres of pristine coastal prairie stretched from the Texas Coastal Bend into Louisiana. Now less than one percent remains. The rest has been lost to farming, grazing, and development.

Many wildflowers are perennials with underground structures such as rhizomes, tubers, crowns or dense mats of intertwined roots. Disturbances to these systems allow competing grasses and plants to quickly replace native prairie vegetation. The U.S. Fish and Wildlife Service and other conservation organizations list the Coastal Prairie as a "critically imperiled ecosystem."

Shafer Garden

At first, Alfred Shafer wasn't sure what to do with the field of prairie grass surrounding his coastal retreat on Baffin Bay near Kingsville. However, when it burst into a vivid palette of color in the spring, he enjoyed the wildflowers so much that he decided to let them grow.

The coastal prarie grasses and wildflowers surrounding Al Shafer's retreat on Baffin Bay provide vital habitat for birds, butterflies, dragonflies, and mammals.

Over the years, Al learned that the secret to beautiful wildflowers in the Texas Coastal Bend is not to mow from the first of December through the middle of May. "That gives the wildflowers plenty of time to flower and reseed."

The most effective wildflower horticulture mimics nature. Plantings of a single species don't do well. Prairies are most stable when natural combinations of grasses, legumes, and wildflowers are encouraged. In subtle symbiosis, the varieties complement each other, form better ground cover, and are healthier, hardier, and more drought resistant.

Al also mows his neighbors' yards. Together they have approximately four acres of wildflowers. They have counted more than eighteen varieties including several types of black-eyed susans, Indian paintbrushes, Indian blankets, and a mix of other wildflowers in pinks, blues, and yellows. "The Winter Texans are always stopping to take photos," he says.

Located near the southern end of the Coastal Bend, the Shafer property exemplifies the subtle ecological transition between the South Texas Brush County and Coastal Prairie and Marshes. Its proximity to the water and presence of grassy fields make it technically part of the Coastal Prairie and Marshes. However, plants characteristic of the Brush Country are also present such as thickets of thorn brush and agave. On the Shafers' property, a few strategically placed cow skulls add to the effect.

Like the Coastal Prairie, the South Texas Brush Country is considered an endangered habitat. This arid forest of prickly brush provides food and shelter to a diverse range of birds, reptiles, and mammals. Mesquite trees moderate the environment beneath their canopies creating microenvironments where granjeno and other native shrubs can grow. The dense woody cover provides shade and cooler temperatures, critical to the

Bobcat rescued by Al Shafer's son

survival of quail, javelina, armadillo, and other native animals during the long hot summers. Coyotes, bobcats, and mountain lions occasionally still can be found where large acreages of thorn forest remain. South Texas is also the last stronghold for federally endangered ocelot and jaguarundi, although sightings of both wildcats continue to decline as their habitat disappears.

At Baffin Bay, they regularly see quail, and cottontails. Al says that his son also finds injured animals such as javelina, deer, and raccoons in the area. He brings them home, cares for them and then releases them back to the wild. ❧

The Shafers' property exemplifies the transition from thorny brush country to coastal prairie.

Krenek Garden

Trees are scarce on most of the Coastal Plains. However, on the northern end of the Texas Coastal Bend near the shoreline there are groves of live oaks surrounded by sandy grasslands called *oak mottes*.

Marsha and Harry Krenek admired the ancient, windswept oaks while vacationing near Rockport, and ultimately decided to retire there. They purchased an undeveloped lot on a small bluff overlooking Copano Bay. The property was still in its native state but scheduled to be brush-hogged.

A biologist, Marsha understood the relationship between plants and wildlife. Therefore, rather than clearing the undergrowth, the Kreneks made a conscious decision to cut as little of the native habitat as possible.

They built their home in a natural clearing and used hand tools to gently prune the understory. Marsha explains, "The understory is the small trees, brush and other vegetation that grows beneath the larger trees. It provides both food and shelter to the wildlife."

A wooden walkway winds through the wildscape of the Kreneks' property down to Copano Bay. The boardwalk protects delicate roots from being trampled by frequent footsteps.

The Kreneks have found that by preserving the natural habitat and learning to live with nature, they are rewarded everyday with something new. Hummingbirds, kiskadees, goldfinches, cardinals, and other birds fill the trees every spring and fall as they pause to rest during their migration along the North American Flyway. ❧

Pale lavender phlox (far left and below) and yellow retama tree blossoms (left) are just a few of the many native flowers found on the Kreneks' property overlooking Copano Bay.

The Kreneks' property is a popular site on the Rockport Hummer/Bird Festival tour which is held every September.

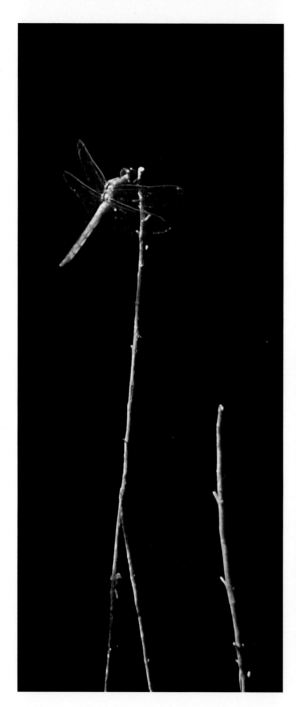

Reemsnyder Garden

Curtis and Anna Reemsnyder's home near Rockport lies at the end of a rough dirt road on Live Oak Peninsula. When they retired, Curtis wanted to find a piece of property with a pond. However, when they finally found one, it was on a lot where everything had been removed except the mature oaks.

"Without the understory, all that was left under the oaks was blowing sand and burr grass," said Anna.

As both Master Gardeners and Master Naturalists, Curtis and Anna decided to restore the property to how it would have been two hundred years ago, before being altered by man.

In prehistoric times, Live Oak Peninsula was a barrier island. Anna describes the local ecology as an efficient, delicately balanced system of big oaks sheltering smaller trees, plants, grasses and wildflowers. Without the protective canopy of trees and understory plants, topsoil quickly blows away, leaving only sand.

The Reemsnyders' pond offers a haven for dragonflies and other wildlife.

The Reemsnyders worked to put back native understory species such as bay trees, yaupon, and American beautyberry. Once established, Anna says these plants are evergreen and easy to care for. The result is a lush and nearly maintenance-free garden.

Now they are adding more flowering plants such as wildflowers and colorful vines to attract additional birds and butterflies . ❧

Above a rustic storage shed is surrounded by threadleaf coreopsis. Other flowering plants found on the Reemsnyders' property include gaillardia (far upper left), pink trumpet vine (far lower left), and passion flowers (left).

Fowler Garden

Jim and Annette Fowler dreamed of a pond where their grandchildren and others could enjoy fishing. Their solution was to dredge one in the field behind their home. After it was completed, Annette encouraged Jim to "make it more interesting." So, he built a bridge resembling the one immortalized in the paintings of Claude Monet, Annette's favorite impressionist artist.

A willow tree, along with mallards, geese, and other migratory waterfowl complete the idyllic setting. The Fowlers planted a kaleidoscope of wildflowers around the pond including coreopsis, Indian blankets, cowpen daisies, and wild orchids. Anna's favorite is the blue-eyed grass, a native wildflower of the Coastal Prairie.

Annette recommends gardeners consider the natural contours and features of their property when planning their gardens. It is much easier to work with the lay of the land than against it. For example, a low spot that collects water makes a good location for a pond or bog garden but could be detrimental to many other types of plants.

For the Fowlers, gazing at the pond and wildflowers has an almost magical calming effect at the end of a long day. ❧

Winecups cascading from a terra cotta urn
raise the spirits, while a sign post
encourages visitors to relax on a bench
surrounded by threadleaf coreopsis.

Olson Garden

Behind the tall, vine-covered wall enclosing the Olson's backyard is a garden full of plumeria, hibiscus, angel trumpets, and ferns. Fern Olson was born and raised in Hawaii. So when she and her husband, Ole, moved to Rockport, she was delighted to be living where she could grow tropicals. She even had the oval swimming pool in the backyard filled to give her more room to plant.

Not long afterwards, they bought the lot next door so Fern could expand her garden further. They refer to the adjacent property as the "outside garden." Fern designed it to attract birds and butterflies. There is always something blooming: passion flowers, morning glories, four o'clocks, zinnias, Mexican petunias, duranta, pink sage, confederate roses, butterfly weed, lion's ear, yucca, turk's cap, honeysuckle, and more.

In addition to wildlife attracted by the flowers, there are other creatures, sculpted by Fern, to be found among the plants. Several years ago, when she couldn't find the type of planters she wanted for her potted plants, she decided to make her own. She used a primitive process similar to raku pottery that combines the basic elements of earth, water, and fire.

Impressed by Fern's artwork, her friends encouraged her to make more, and before long her pottery was being sold at the local art gallery. Today, Fern and sixteen other local artists operate an art co-op, The Gallery of Rockport, in downtown Rockport.

The personality of Fern's "Garden Head" sculptures change with the type of plant used as "hair." A rat-tail cactus conjures images of Medusa. Ferns, bougainvillea or bromeliads create wood nymphs or seductive aliens. ❧

Original garden sculpture by Fern Olson

Tree frog perched on yucca

Sculpted head among angel trumpets

Turk's cap (left) and
Tea Hibiscus (below)

A rat-tail cactus planted in Fern Olson's "Garden Head" sculpture conjures images of Medusa.

ISLAND LIVING

A string of long, narrow islands protects the bays and shores of the Coastal Bend from the pounding surf of the open Gulf. Padre Island, the world's longest barrier island, parallels the Laguna Madre, extending 113 miles from the Rio Grande delta to Corpus Christi Bay. Across the mouth of the bay lies Mustang Island. To the north, St. Joseph and Matagorda islands protect Aransas, Copano and San Antonio Bays. The barrier islands were formed 5,000 to 8,000 years ago following a rise in sea level caused by melting glaciers. Remnants of an even older island chain are found along the mainland.

Sandy soils, coastal winds and salty sea spray make gardening a challenge on the islands and along the bays. At the same time, nearby coastal waters moderate temperatures, giving gardeners the opportunity to experiment with tropical foliage and exotic plants which might freeze in other areas of the Coastal Bend.

Dunn Garden

The Rockport community of Key Allegro is located on a small man-made island in Aransas Bay. Like many island neighborhoods, the homes are built along canals with backyard landscapes designed to be enjoyed from the water as well as the back decks.

Priscilla and Jerry Dunn went a step further in creating their backyard vista. When Key Allegro began filling with tall houses, they became concerned that their view would be spoiled, so they bought the lot across the canal to preserve the green space.

There, Priscilla created *En Plein Aire Palette*, an open-air palette of color to inspire artists. In creating the garden, she mixed topsoil and organic matter into existing soil. She also was careful to use plants which adapt well to local conditions. As a result, salt water and sea air have not caused any problems, and her garden is fairly self-sustaining.

The Dunns' backyard overlooks *En Plein Aire Palette* across the canal.

Varied views of *En Plein Aire Palette* garden.

"You don't have to use exotic plants to create the look of a traditional, formal garden," said Priscilla.

"Everything keeps growing without much effort on my part. I just keep things cut back and in shape. It's my therapy. It relaxes me."

En Plein Aire Palette blooms spectacularly year round with cerise-colored bougainvillea, red pentas, and brightly-hued hibiscus. Dwarf white oleanders create a fence along the street, and Mexican petunias cover the slope along the water.

The garden around the Dunns' home is equally wonderful with indigo spire salvia blowing in the wind beside the bulkhead, and bougainvillea trailing from the upper story of the house. Priscilla has made abundant use of herbs in the beds around her home. Oregano, she says, makes a good ground cover that doesn't require a lot of care and is pest-free. Provence lavender likes dry conditions and fills the air with its delicate perfume.

In protecting their own view, the Dunns' have benefited their entire community by providing beautifully landscaped gardens on both sides of the canal. ❀

An Armillary sphere sundial clock adds interest to the Dunns' backyard.

Indigo spire salvia and other plants border the bulkhead.

Chancellor Garden

"No one, except an island person, understands the challenge of the wind and sand," says Carolyn Chancellor.

Before Carolyn and her husband, Robert, moved to Port Aransas, she was involved with the Native Plant Society in Houston. But, climate and soil conditions were entirely different there.

So when the Chancellors arrived in Port Aransas in 1993, Carolyn asked what plants would grow well on the island. She was given a list of twelve plants.

"I knew there had to be more!"

Determined, she turned her garden into "one big experiment." Whenever she traveled, she brought back at least one plant that might work in the sandy, windy, dry conditions of the island.

Other members of the Port Aransas Garden Club and the Native Plant Society also worked to find and experiment with plants. Together they compiled a list of more than two hundred island-suitable plants and wrote a book on gardening in Port Aransas.

Having identified a wide selection of plants that adapt well to the harsh climate of the island, Carolyn's yard is now a mixture of Texas natives and non-native tropicals. Carolyn's next goal is to turn her "hodgepodge of plants" into a planned landscape. ❧

Coral vine, or queen's wreath, blooms profusely along the Chancellors' back deck.

The delicate looking shell ginger blossoms
attract buff-bellied hummingbirds and tree frogs.

An oval bed overflows with colorful plants such as cosmos
and Mexican bush sage that are capable of tolerating the
sand, heat and wind of Mustang Island.

Fucik Garden

Dr. John Fucik's home on Mustang Island sits on a sand dune a thousand feet behind the high tide line of the Gulf of Mexico. Terraced beds climb the dunes that abut his backyard. He constructed the terraces from recycled materials such as railroad ties, concrete blocks, and tires to hold the dunes in place and provide a place to garden. The terraces are capped with rustic fences woven from oleander branches to provide a windbreak and dam the soil.

A retired horticulture professor, John designed the beds so that there would be a transition from cultivated beds on the lower level to wilder, native plantings of sea oats, camphor weed, and wild phlox towards the top and then ultimately to the natural dune. Because sand does not hold water or nutrients well, he lined the beds with building paper and filled them with a mixture of sand, soil, and organic matter.

Over the years, he has tested the ability of various plants to survive the conditions on the Gulf side of the island. The greatest challenge he has encountered is the wind because it strips plants of their foliage. John says that the island's high water table also presents a problem for deep-rooted plants. ❧

◀ Terraced beds behind Dr. John Fucik's home on Mustang Island.

Page Garden

Upon waking, Shirlee Page likes to gaze across the wetlands behind the home that she and her husband, Paul, built on the bay side of Mustang Island.

She recalls, "This morning there was a flock of roseate spoonbills, and I thought, 'Another day in paradise'."

The Pages' garden paradise is filled with tropical blooms. A colorful array of plumeria, hibiscus, bougainvillea, and oleanders are mixed with a variety of native species. She says she loves the colors and look of the tropicals, but wanted native plants to attract and feed the birds.

The Pages took special care to select plants that would minimize water usage. "That ruled out a large lawn," says Shirlee. She says using organic mulch is her secret to a low maintenance yard. It helps retain moisture, reduces weeds, and keeps the soil well-conditioned. She tries to avoid chemicals because of their negative effects on the bay waters, birds and other wildlife.

In planning her garden, Shirlee watched where the sun traveled so she could determine where the shade would be at different times of the day. Even though there are few shade trees on the island, shadows cast by nearby houses affect how well plants do in different areas.

According to Shirlee, wind and heat are the biggest challenges gardeners face on the island. "But if you select the right plants, they do surprisingly well."

A large firecracker plant attracts butterflies and hummingbirds to the Pages' backyard.

Schall Garden

Like many homes on North Padre Island, Edie and Thomas Schall's backyard overlooks a busy canal. The front yard is their private garden retreat.

On cool evenings, a fire dances in a *chimenea* behind the white stucco walls that conceal the front of the house. The pleasant aroma of smoke blends with rosemary and jasmine, while the sound of water soothes.

In designing their courtyard garden, the Schalls wanted

The walls around the front of the house provide privacy and block out the noise of the street.

to create a place of solace that would require little upkeep. They recruited the services of a professional landscaper, who helped them choose plants that were slow-growing and low-maintenance. They avoided plants that tend to shed petals such as hibiscus and oleanders.

Many of the cacti are from the Schalls' previous home in Tucson. The Arizona-style Xeriscape keeps watering, pruning, and other gardening chores to a minimum. Edie says caring for the plants requires no more than an hour each week. The low-maintenance frees them to travel without concern for their garden.

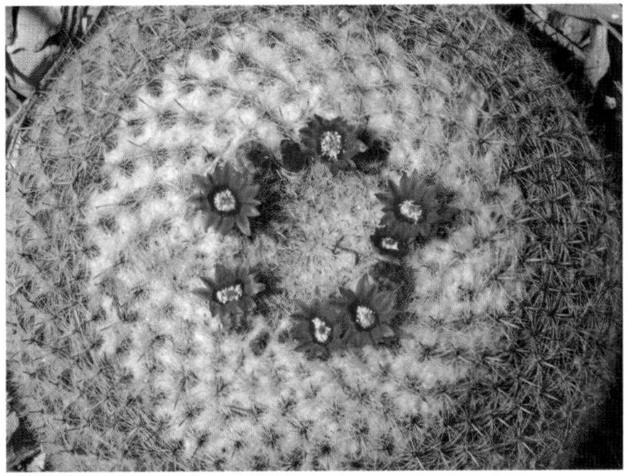

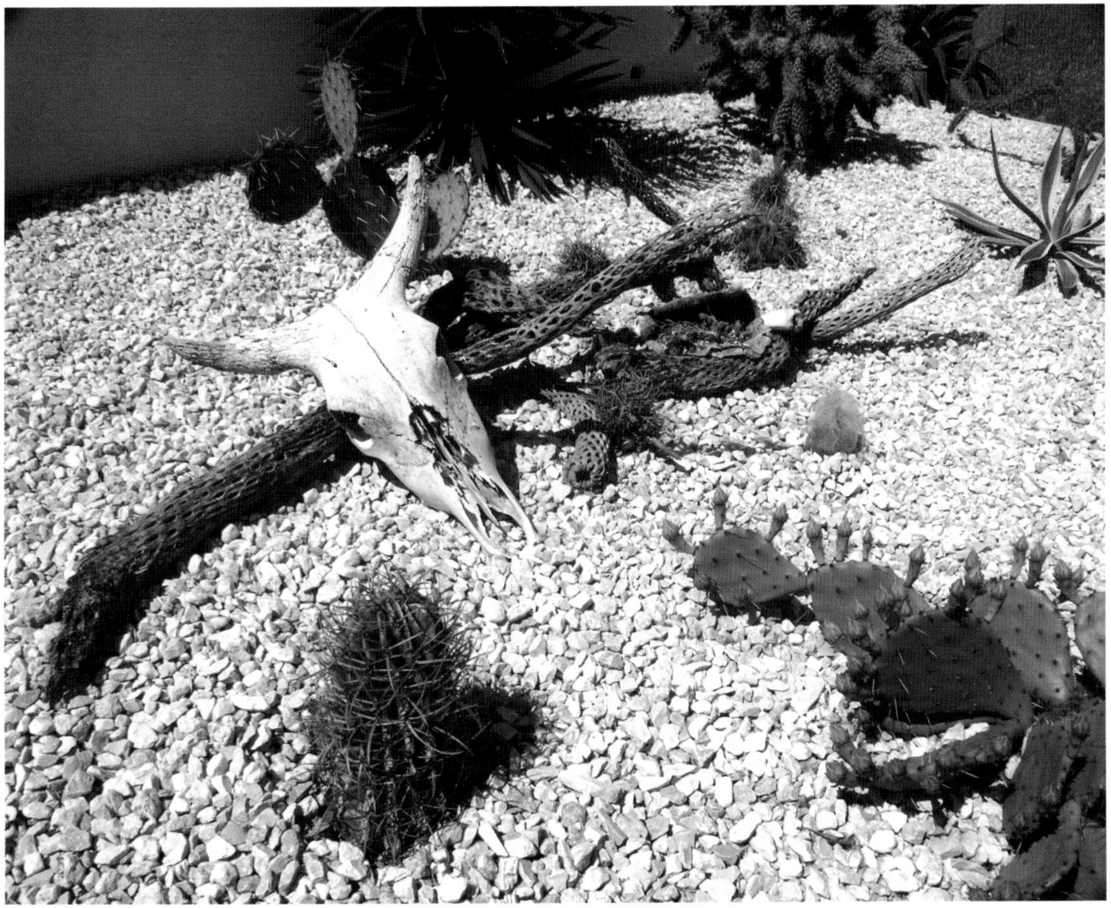

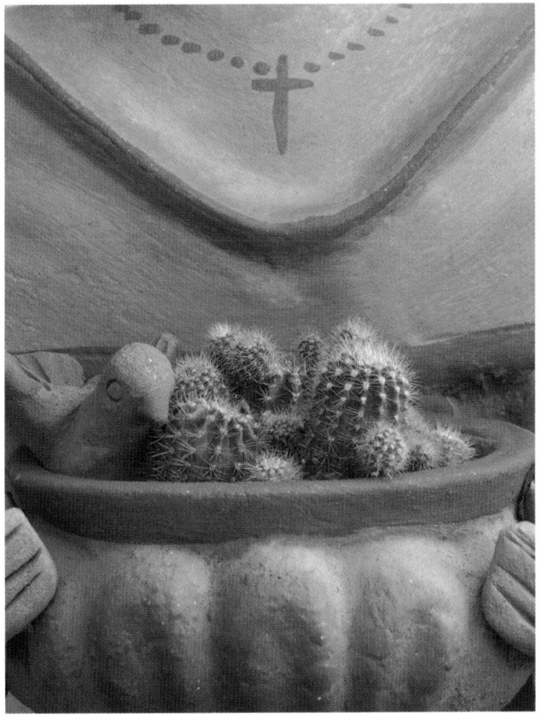

Pincushion cactus (top right) and echinocereus cactus (above).

A cow skull and cholla cactus wood are surrounded by prickly pear, variegated agave, and fishhook cactus (left).

WATERWISE GARDENING

Wise use of water is critical in South Texas. The award-winning Xeriscape Learning Center and Design Garden located at the Corpus Christi Museum of Science and History demonstrates how seven simple principles can result in beautiful landscapes while conserving water. They are: (1) planning and design, (2) soil analysis, (3) appropriate plant selection, (4) practical turf areas, (5) efficient irrigation, (6) use of mulch, and (7) appropriate maintenance.

Simply adding mulch around existing plants reduces surface evaporation, moderates soil temperatures, and reduces weeds. Adjusting watering schedules, using drip irrigation or large water droplet producing sprinkler heads helps reduce the amount of water lost to evaporation.

Incorporating drought tolerant grass varieties like Bermudagrass and Floratam in place of traditional St. Augustine lawns is another step to reducing lawn water use.

Homeowners do not have to sacrifice color to save water. Stroll through the

Aloe vera flower spikes soar over trailing rosemary.

Drought hardy Texas sage blooms after a summer rain shower.

Xeriscape Garden and you will see many colorful South Texas natives such as Texas sage, Texas mountain laurel, and dwarf Barbados cherry next to tropical Turk's cap, esperanza, shell ginger, Mexican honeysuckle, and Asian jasmine. To help gardeners identify plants that are proven performers in the Corpus Christi area, local garden centers have adopted a purple water-wise plant label system. ❧

A winding wall of recycled sidewalks lining the backside of a man-made berm adds height and interest to the flat topography.

Shallow bays and lagoons trapped behind low islands characterize the South Texas coastline. The largest of the bays is the broad crescent-shaped Corpus Christi Bay.

Skinner Garden

On its northern shore lies the City of Portland where Barbara and Tom Skinners' waterfront home overlooks the deepest part of the bay. Reminiscent of a Mexican hacienda, the Skinners' home is guarded by a tall white wall and iron gate. The only hint of what lies beyond is a small sign that reads "My Garden."

"When we built the house in 1990, we began with a lawn and flowerbeds, because that's what everyone did," said Barbara. "However, our original dream was to have an atrium entrance full of plants."

Within a few years, the coastal climate had taken its toll on the lawn, and Barbara decided the grass had to come out. She replaced it with *saltillo* tile and raised planter boxes where she could have an old-fashioned garden full of colors which would change with the seasons.

Today, the planter boxes are overflowing and the Skinners have the atrium courtyard they desired. Developing the garden has taken time: time to study

the landscape to determine where plants will fit best and time to mature the plants. Most of Barbara's plants have come from cuttings and bulbs given to her by friends who said, "Put this in your garden and see if it grows."

Barbara identifies her plants by the names of friends who gave them. In spring, the stately, yellow

"Edith Iris" reigns over begonias, impatiens, petunias, salvia, roses, and larkspur. By June, the courtyard changes into a hot summer garden full of hibiscus, orchids, bougainvillas, chrysanthemums, and zinnias. Many blooms last through autumn into winter, when they are complemented by nasturtiums, impatiens, and johnny-jump-ups.

Confederate jasmine covers the gate to the Skinners' garden.

Barbara does not use any chemical fertilizers or pesticides. Instead, she takes an organic approach to gardening so as not to harm the bay or visiting wildlife.

"If there is an invasion of insects, I don't worry. It will pass," she says. "Gardening should not be a worry, but a joy."

Her garden is filled with wasps, bees, and birds. One morning, she says a hummingbird paused to sip nectar from a bundle of cut flowers she was carrying in her arms.

In the evening, Barbara spends time watering and admiring her flowers. One senses that what makes her garden bloom so profusely is not the work she puts into it, but the love. She says she doesn't "work" in her garden, "I simply make it possible for things to grow."

Cattelya 'Bob Betts' orchid

Yellow irises reign over the Skinners' spring garden where newcomers and old friends alike are compelled to stop and admire the colorful array of blooms.

A yellow jacket rests on a yellow iris.

Ocean House

Ocean Drive

The City of Corpus Christi's distinctive skyline sweeps across the western shore of Corpus Christi Bay. In the late 1930s Guzon Borglum, sculptor of Mount Rushmore, worked with the city to beautify its waterfront. He designed a stepped seawall to connect the cityscape with the open water. Fill material was pumped behind the wall to create a scenic boulevard along the shoreline. Borglum envisioned an avenue lined with majestic palms extending from Corpus Christi to the Rio Grande Valley. Although this ambitious project was never realized, Borglum's vision of a landscaped boulevard bordering Corpus Christi Bay did.

Ocean Drive is considered to be one of the most beautiful residential drives in Texas. Gracious mansions interspersed with public parks line the thoroughfare. Early development began in 1890 when visionary developer Elihu H. Ropes arrived in Corpus Christi full of ideas for turning the sleepy little town into a tourist mecca. In 1891, he constructed a magnificent 125-room hotel on a prominent bluff overlooking the bay and planned to surround it with an exclusive residential area. He named the luxury hotel Alta Vista, Spanish for "high view." The Alta Vista Hotel never opened due to a recession that dried up Rope's financial resources. The elaborate structure ultimately burned in 1927 in a spectacular fire.

Street names like Alta Plaza, Rossiter and Ropes remained and the neighborhoods along Ocean Drive became choice locations for the city's most prestigious homes. Across from where the Alta Vista Hotel once stood, visitors to Corpus Christi have an opportunity to experience the elegance of living in one of these homes at the Ocean House. Built in 1936 and currently listed as a bed and breakfast, Ocean House is a spacious, Mediterranean-styled retreat surrounded by a luxurious garden filled with nearly forty species of tropical flowers. ❧

Campbell Garden

The sprawling waterside home of Dr. Charles and Mary Campbell was built in 1937. Mary says her favorite room is the pool house because it allows her to bring the outdoors indoors.

Mary has a deep appreciation for nature and has created a habitat for migratory birds around her home. She has planted oak trees, shrimp plants, and colorful vines such as cape honeysuckle and bougainvillea to attract hummingbirds and other avian visitors. An orchid tree, red bud tree, and muscadine grapevine are original to the property.

Mary says her biggest challenge has been finding things that grow along the water. Some unidentified plants appearing voluntarily she plans to let stay. She says philosophically, "God is the Master Gardener. Where God puts things is where they are supposed to grow."

Orchid tree blossoms

An amaryllis is sillouetted against the window of the pool house.

Guinn Garden

Tending the garden surrounding Dr. Lee and Jane Guinn's home at the corner of Ocean Drive and Del Mar Boulevard is a full-time job. The immense garden covers a city block and is enclosed by a decorative Victorian brick and cast iron fence brought from New Orleans.

The Mediterranean-style mansion was built in the 1930s for Frank and Marie Crook. In order to create a garden in the style of the Old South, the Crooks had fill dirt brought from East Texas to raise the level of the yard nearly five feet. The deep layer of acidic soil enabled them to grow towering magnolias and luxuriant azaleas. A plumeria planted by the Crooks in the 1940s still thrives and is thought to be the largest in town.

The Crooks added a metal and glass conservatory and greenhouse to the northwest corner of the property in 1942. Lord and Burnham, a firm that normally built greenhouses for universities, designed one for the Crooks with sunburst windows over the French doors. The greenhouses originally were used primarily for growing orchids. Today, they also house a variety of plants including bromeliads and birds of paradise.

Several eye-catching topiaries are located in a sculpture garden on the north side of the property. The topiaries were bought in Houston already formed. Once mature, maintenance of topiaries is much like any other shrub. They require water, food and regular trimming. The most difficult challenge is maintaining the shape.

Glimpses behind the wall of the Guinns' Ocean Drive home.

Across the back of the Guinn's house, a curved walkway is flanked by a bank of azaleas that bloom profusely in the dappled shade. Citrus trees including, orange, lime and grapefruit, flourish near the greenhouse. Nearby, around the large tiled swimming pool, is a trellis covered in passion vine. At the back end of the pool, a blue wall dividing the guest house from the garage displays colorful hand-painted wooden fish. Gardening consultant Carol Bush says when she looks at old photos of the house she can see how the garden has changed slightly from one owner to the next, each change reflecting different styles and preferences. ❧

Passion Flower

Kalanchoe

Ramos Garden

Dr. Alvaro and Carmen Ramos call their house their dream home. They wanted a place where they always would feel as if they were vacationing in a tropical paradise. So, they designed the house so that each room offers a panoramic view of Corpus Christi Bay, and the front windows overlook a lush tropical garden.

Originally from Colombia, both Carmen and Alvaro love tropical plants and flowers. But, having lived in Corpus Christi for more than 30 years, they knew the challenges the climate posed to tender vegetation. Therefore, they specifically requested their architect design the house "with open arms to protect the plants from north winds."

Walls and contours of the front wings replicate the protective canopy of a tropical forest. Beneath tall palms, colorful crotons, hibiscus, and other tropicals flourish. Recessed areas on either side of the main entrance provide additional protection to more delicate palms, including one the Ramoses nurtured from a coconut brought back from Colombia.

Dr. Ramos says the triangle palms that flank the front doorway normally are not found in Corpus Christi because they will freeze. Theirs, however, have done exceptionally well in the protected microenvironment at the front of their house. Their garden features palms from Guatemala, Mexico, Hawaii, and Colombia.

Carmen and Alvaro also enjoy having a variety of colorful annuals around their home, selected according to season and availability. In winter, they plant mostly impatiens and begonias. In the backyard, pansies, petunias, impatiens and begonias survive well into summer because the house protects them from hot afternoon sun. During the summer, they plant periwinkles, zinnias, and black-eyed daisies in front creating a spectacular display of color for cyclists, motorists, and joggers to enjoy as they travel along Ocean Drive. ◆

◀ A brilliant display of colorful annuals and tropical palms create a vacation-like setting on Corpus Christi Bay.

"Water is Life" is inscribed on fountains around the world. In hot, arid climates, water features are the heart of a garden. They add interest and cooling serenity. No longer limited to concrete figures spitting water, water features take the form of birdbaths, fountains, ponds, still pools, fanciful sprays, or rippling cascades. They can be simple or highly intricate and creative.

Water features provide an avenue for art to be incorporated into both public and private gardens. Next to the Art Center of Corpus Christi, a set of sculptures titled "Crossing the Stream" grace the park along Shoreline Drive. The pond is an integral part of both the artist's work and the park's landscape. It also plays a key role in subliminally suggesting a cooling effect to visitors and provides a welcome retreat from the heat of the South Texas sun in mid-summer. The park and pond were a gift to the city from philanthropist Dusty Durrill in 2002. He saw the lost wax bronze sculpture in a publication and was charmed by the children. Designed by Italian sculptor, Leonard Rossi, the bronze playmates are named Giuseppe, Mario, Antonio, Luisa, and Rosa. ❧

"Crossing the Stream" at the Art Center of Corpus Christi

Creveling Garden

Inside the garden entryway leading to John and Judy Creveling's home, an unusual three-part fountain commemorates trees. Water trickling down rough granite columns enhances the dimensions of sight and sound. Designed and built in 1997 by renowned sculptor Jesus Moroles, the "Column Fountains" are included in the book, *Moroles Granite Sculptures*, along with his many other works displayed throughout the world. Moroles, who serves on the board of the Smithsonian Art Museum, resides in Rockport.

A decorative waterspout resembling a Mexican *canal*, or roof gutter, adds interest to the Mexican-style swimming pool designed by landscape architect Thomas H. Walsh for the Crevelings.

Roberts Garden

Water features do not have to be expensive or elaborate to transform a simple garden into an inviting oasis. Nancy Roberts used her ingenuity to turn a heavy antique French lard urn purchased at an antique shop into an attractive fountain. After persuading a local glass company to drill a hole in the bottom, Nancy bought a fountain kit with a small pump and assembled the fountain herself. She says the process was fairly simple. The result is a lovely garden display which conjures images of a young maid leaving her overturned water vessel while she rests a few moments from her chores.

Males Garden

A large saltwater pool provides a stunning focal point for Deborah and Gary Males' beautiful garden located on a double lot near Ocean Drive. Deborah says that the elements of *feng shui* came together naturally in their pool landscape. They wanted a waterfall to spill over into the pool. To design the shape, they used a garden hose to outline shadows from the mesquite trees at five o'clock in the afternoon. The pool was built by Bruce Owen of Artisan Pools using a retro-system called Mineral Springs, which Deborah says is less harsh to hair and skin and less expensive to operate.

Oshman & Riordan Garden

Porticos and covered walkways bring the outdoors in at the canal side home of Sandra Oshman and Rick Riordan in Port Aransas. Inside the arched entryway, a Mexican fountain welcomes visitors. In the backyard, an unusual design turns a swimming pool into an eye-catching water feature.

Meadows Garden

Water gardens range in form and size from whiskey barrels to elaborate ponds that encompass much of the landscape. They embody all the elements of other water features plus the aspect of being living ecosystems.

When Dr. Mary Meadows began landscaping her property in Rockport, she envisioned a pond filled with ducks, fish and waterlilies. She had a large pond dug and filled with goldfish, waterlilies and other aquatic plants. She says herons soon ate the goldfish, and some of the aquatic plants became invasive. At that time, there were few sources of information on water gardens so much of Mary's early efforts were trial and error. Fortunately, she says, the increasing popularity of water gardens resulted in the formation of a Pond Club and she since has learned more about creating and managing pond ecosystems. ❧

Exotic waterlilies are a staple of many water gardens with their floating leaves and colorful blooms emerging from the water.

Nuss Garden

Patty and Hank Nuss enjoy the tranquil sound of water trickling in the background and have incorporated several water features into their garden. Next to a gazebo, a small waterfall flows into a flagstone-lined pond.

The Nusses' large, mature yard was originally designed with enormous, deep flowerbeds that required constant care. After purchasing the home, the Nusses decided to redesign the backyard. A landscape architect helped them define the perimeters of the yard using brick walkways and low walls. He also helped engineer their remarkable combination spa and fountain. Turn the control knobs one way, and water is forced through side jets for a relaxing spa. Turn the knobs another way, and water is forced up into the air to create a dramatic fountain. In the evening, lights add to the drama. ❧

A small pond edged with limestone is tucked near the far end of the Nuss's gazebo (right). Potted impatiens and begonias border a combination spa and fountain (below).

Julie's Backyard Bistro

Hidden behind a deceptively ordinary home, on a narrow rural lane between Aransas Pass and Rockport, is an extraordinary garden where all are welcome. Chef Julie Olson-Price conceived the idea of creating a greenhouse dining room in her backyard in the early 1990s. After two and a half years of planning, permitting and construction, the restaurant opened in 1994 as Julie's Backyard Bistro. It is now one of the premier gourmet restaurants in the Coastal Bend.

The garden is an integral part of the restaurant's cuisine and ambience. Guests enter the greenhouse dining room across an arched bridge over a small pond landscaped with waterlilies, cannas, and bearded irises. The courtyard dining area is adorned with palm trees, roses, and dahlias as well as Asiatic, oriental and gloriosa lilies. There also is a variety of herbs which Julie picks fresh each day for the restaurant. Dining is a relaxed, leisurely experience where each guest's meal is individually prepared from scratch by Julie and garnished with fresh flowers and herbs.

Julie says that maintaining her garden is not "labor" to her. Instead, it is something that she would do anyway for her own pleasure and enjoyment. ✺

Julie Olson-Price embedded broken plates, shells, bottles and bits of pottery in the wall surrounding the pond (left). The dahlias she planted do well in dappled sun (below right). Her garden is also full of amaryllis, lilies, and other bulbs (bottom right).

An arched bridge leads to the entrance of the greenhouse dining room at Julie's Backyard Bistro.

Sentz Garden

Beyond the charming cottage gate leading to Geralyn and Richard Sentz's backyard, a flagstone path wanders through a spectacular display of garden color. Drawing inspiration from the Texas Hill Country, Geralyn started with a pond and a small patio attached to the house. They extended the patio to create an inviting spot for enjoying the outdoors. Then they enlarged the pond and surrounded it with hill country stone.

Geralyn says that when she first started gardening she used "trial and error;" but after losing several plants she decided to read more about what grows well in South Texas. Today, the Sentz's garden is a favorite spot on area garden tours. Geralyn says May is the best time to view her garden. "Everything is in bloom." Her secret to the profusion of flowers is keeping the plants trimmed.

"After the 2002 Garden Tour, people would come to the door and ask if they could show my garden to their friend, or sister, or mother," Geralyn recalls. "They said they remembered it from the tour and wanted to use some of the ideas in their own garden. That makes me feel good." ❧

Barnette Garden

Like many Corpus Christi homes, Joyce and Jim Barnette's front yard has a traditional lawn with a few trees. The backyard, however, is a lush, private landscape that Joyce began developing more than thirty years ago.

"I like lots of color. I also don't like to have lots of the same thing;" therefore she changes her garden with the seasons. She enjoys cleaning out beds and planting something new. Joyce says Jim isn't a gardener, but "he enjoys a pretty yard so he doesn't mind my frequent trips to the nursery to buy plants. I like finding something new to plant in my flower beds."

After thirty years, her garden is still evolving.

A whimsical clay sculpture hangs from a tree, and impatiens fill a toy wagon (above).

◄ A water girl sits surrounded by a sea of Mexican heather, impatiens and Easter lilies.

Burt Garden

Joy and Ron Burt make an industrious, innovative team. Ron does the pathways and garden structures, and Joy takes care of the plants. Together they have created a pleasant backyard retreat with more than 130 different plants.

They began with a fishpond. After landscaping around the pond, Joy decided that it looked so good she would add a little more. She kept adding and adding until "pretty soon there wasn't much grass left."

The Burts' garden is filled with flowering plants: plumbago, rock rose, Mexican sage, Mexican petunias, roses, blue daze, marigolds, and other annuals.

"Soil preparation is the most important thing for a healthy garden. I use lots of good compost and topsoil," Joy emphasized.

The idea to add the pergola came while standing in line at a home and garden store. Thumbing through a magazine, the Burts saw a photo of a pergola they liked. Ron said "I can build that!" Since then, Ron also has built arbors, trellises, birdhouses, and pathways.

Now that everything is established, Joy still finds plenty to do. She is always transplanting or replacing plants. "Gardens are ongoing. They are never finished."

Krejci Garden

Martha Krejci says that up until the early 1990s, her backyard in Calallen consisted of a vegetable garden, a large barbeque pit, a boat, and a metal shed.

Then she visited the Antique Rose Store in Brenham and was amazed that "something like that could grow in Texas."

She came home and began transforming her yard into an English cottage garden. She and her husband replaced the metal shed with a wooden one. He added a deck and trellis, and painted it yellow with white trim. She built the pathway, and planted annuals around the cottage and under the trees. Little by little, the garden grew.

Eventually Martha replaced the vegetable garden with a rose garden. "There were always more vegetables than we could eat or give away at one time," she said. "Roses, I can give away year-round, and they are always appreciated."

To learn more about growing roses, she joined the Corpus Christi Rose Society. Later, she took the Master Gardener class.

Martha plants mostly annuals and replaces them each season to keep color year-round. In the fall, she has chrysanthemums and oxalis. In the spring, there are geraniums, begonias, impatiens, petunias, and gerbera daisies.

"I love all types of flowers," she says, smiling. "But roses are my favorites. I have a bouquet on my kitchen table almost year-round. The fragrance is wonderful."

Alyssum and verbena complement roses.

Catenazzo Garden

Joe Catenazzo's backyard reflects the influences of his early travels and a lifelong passion for flowers. Born in New York, he enjoyed going to the Brooklyn Botanic Garden as a child to see the tulips. While he was still young, his family moved to Puerto Rico. There he fell in love with hibiscus and other tropicals. Upon returning to New York, he found the city a gray, dreary place except for a nearby "postage stamp-size garden overflowing with roses."

It was in Italy that Joe found heaven. The mild, sunny climate and cool evenings were wonderful for roses. There were large nurseries to explore and beautiful pottery to be found.

Joe's family moved to Corpus Christi in 1981, where he found growing flowers takes time and patience. Despite these challenges, Joe has a yard full of colorful blooms year round. He says roses are his favorite because one bush produces so many beautiful flowers, and they are so versatile and fragrant.

On foggy days, Joe enjoys the ethereal feel of his garden. ▶

The subtropical climate of the Coastal Bend allows gardeners to grow a diverse array of plants. Roses, plumeria, palms, succulents, daylilies, and even orchids and bromeliads are becoming commonplace in local gardens. These specialty plants often ignite a passion in gardeners, who then actively seek to find and share information about their plant of interest.

Garden clubs and plant societies provide guidance and inspiration to novice and experienced gardeners, as well as opportunities to socialize with like-minded gardening enthusiasts. Local plant societies now include the rose, orchid, plumeria, bromeliad, cacti and succulent, African violet, daylily, palm, and native plant societies, as well as the bonsai and water garden clubs. The oldest local plant society still in existence in our area is the Corpus Christi Rose Society, founded in 1955.

The tall, free blooming and fragrant *Louise Estes* is an excellent show rose.

The *Brilliant Pink Iceberg* is a sport of the iceberg rose.

ROSES

Roses are a favorite of many gardeners, though not all roses do well in South Texas. To help local gardeners select and care for roses, members of the Corpus Christi Rose Society volunteer at local nurseries each winter to provide tips on growing roses. According to Rose Society member Jan Shannon, "Growing roses is like raising kids. They thrive on a schedule of proper care, nutrition, and protection."

Properly cared for, roses bloom nine months out of the year in the Coastal Bend. Gardeners from the north often are surprised to learn that due to the heat, summer is when roses become dormant in South Texas rather than winter. ❧

The hand-painted *George Burns* rose is one of rosarian Jan Shannon's favorites. "It is a hand-painted variety," she explains. "Like snowflakes, no two are alike."

Orchids

Orchids fascinate many people with their exotic shapes, wide spectrum of colors and long-lasting blooms. For Rosa Meilleur, tending her orchids and other plants is her favorite pastime. She enjoys trimming, nurturing, finding new blooms, and seeing the changes. Rosa's first orchid was a dendrobium she purchased in 1964. Dendrobiums and phalaenopsis are both good choices for novice growers, offering a wide range of colors, sizes, and shapes. Orchids come in nearly every color of the spectrum except black.

Rosa's greenhouse provides a shaded canopy for her orchids during hot summer months. In winter, she covers it with plastic to keep the plants warm. In the Coastal Bend, orchids also can be grown indoors near a cool window or on a sheltered patio.

At the home of Nina and Herman Johnson, more than seven hundred orchids surround their swimming pool. They began growing orchids more than twenty five years ago. Some of their plants are nearly thirty years old. Together, the Johnsons like to travel worldwide to attend orchid conventions and collect specimens.

Nina says the covered pool creates the ideal climate for orchids–high humidity and moderate temperatures. In the Coastal Bend, orchids bloom best during the cooler months with sprays lasting a month or more if well-tended. Herman claims that his orchids thrive on "negligent care" and do fine for a week with no attention when he is away. ❧

Orchids come in every color of the spectrum except black. Rosa Meilleur's *Chocolate Drop* cattelya orchid, however, comes close.

A *China Dragon 'Orchis'* orchid is a favorite of Nina and Herman Johnson.

Hibiscus

Profuse blooms, an endless variety of colors, and the ability to thrive in high summer temperatures and intense sun make the hibiscus a favorite of many Coastal Bend gardeners. There are numerous species labeled under the 'hibiscus' name, but the term is most often associated with the tropical species, *Hibiscus rosa-sinensis* L., for which there are over 5,000 registered cultivars. The best varieties for Coastal Bend landscapes typically have single blooms with five petals. The full and crested doubles are identical but have extra petals in addition to the basic five. Bloom sizes commonly vary from three to eight inches with even larger sizes appearing on some hybrids. Color combinations and flower forms are extraordinarily mixed in an almost endless variation of shade and petal arrangement with black and true blue being the only hues not currently available. Unfortunately, the bigger and fancier the flower, the fewer blooms there are typically to enjoy.

In 1957 the tropical hibiscus was adopted as the city flower of Corpus Christi to represent the beauty of the city. Many feel the hibiscus was the ideal choice for several reasons. First, the evergreen shrubs are well-suited for the region's semi-tropical climate. Furthermore, its colorful, elegant flowers provide an excellent visual welcome mat to visitors and residents of the Coastal Bend. ❧

The exotic *Ocean Spray* is an elegant tropical hibiscus with bright colors and ruffled edges.

Single bloom hibiscus grow well in the Coastal Bend and are found in an assortment of colors.

Palms

Jana Whalen's passion is palm trees. While spending time on a small island near Thailand, she developed a strong affinity for the image of beaches lined with coconut palms. Later she and her former husband, Gary Meiser, became involved with the International Palm Society and began growing palms. Today, her backyard is filled with a diverse collection of palms, and she is an active member of the Palm Society of South Texas.

One of the local Palm Society's goals is to educate gardeners on the many varieties of palms that grow well in the area. According to Jana, there are more than thirty varieties of palms that easily can withstand the Coastal Bend climate.

Palms are not really trees. They are in a class of their own and include several thousand different species. There are feather-leafed palms and fan-leafed palms, towering single-trunk types and tiny multiple stem ones. Some live in deserts, others on mountain tops, and still others flourish in lush tropical rainforests.

In addition to the beauty and immense diversity of palms, Jana says she likes palms because "they don't take over. They are predictable and easy to maintain." ❧

A Giant Bird of Paradise leans into a Queen palm.

While not a palm,
banana trees are frequently
found in tropical landscapes.

Bottle palm

Purslane thrives at the base of a queen palm

Bromeliads

In international bromeliad circles, the name Anderson is synonymous with bromeliads. At the 15th World Bromeliad Conference, John's *Aechmea biflora* took Best of Show and his *Tillandsia streptophylla* was the Sweepstakes Winner. His wife, Nelwyn, a top bromeliad grower in her own right, earned highest honors in the Single Non-Blooming division with her *Guzmania 'Claret'*. Following John's passing in 2003, the Bromeliad Society International posthumously honored him for his contributions to furthering bromeliad research and cultivation by establishing the *Best Aechmea John Anderson Award* at the 16th World Bromeliad Conference in 2004.

"John loved all bromeliads, but the *Aechmea* was his true passion," says Nelwyn.

Few could have imagined twenty years ago that John's passion would blossom into eight greenhouses covering more than three acres. Hidden behind a small house in a modest Corpus Christi neighborhood, the complex is home to the largest private collection of *Aechmea* species in the world including one named after Anderson, *Aechmea andersonii*. There is also the *Aechmea 'Nelwyn'*, a cultivar of the *Aechmea pedicellata* that John named after his wife.

The Anderson's built their first greenhouse in 1982 so John would have more space to grow bromeliads. One greenhouse quickly became four. Later they bought the property next door and built four more. A mechanical engineer by trade, John designed the greenhouses specifically for bromeliads and devised a system for collecting rain water to water

Aechmea chantinii blooms in the foreground.

Neoregelia 'Katherine'

Aechmea tayoensis

Vrieslansia 'Harmony'

the plants. During droughts, reverse osmosis produces fresh water for the plants.

Nelwyn says that it was during a phone conversation with their son while he was attending Texas A&M University that John coined the name "Epiphitimy Extension Station" for their greenhouse complex. Most bromeliads are epiphytic, taking their nutrition and moisture from the atmosphere.

During his lifetime, John Anderson collected innumerable bromeliads from the jungles of Brazil, Ecuador, and Costa Rica, carefully categorizing and labeling each one. He discovered the *Aechmea andersonii* on an expedition to Brazil in 1997.

Nelwyn has focused much of her attention on growing *Neoregelis,* because of their brilliantly colored leaves, and *cryptanthus,* a terrestrial bromeliad. All bromeliads have a spiral arrangement of leaves called a rosette. The number of degrees between successive leaves varies from species to species. The bases of the leaves in the rosette may overlap tightly to form a water reservoir. This central cup also collects whatever leaf litter and insects happen to land in it, fertilizing the plant.

With few exceptions, the flower stalk, or inflorescence as it is called, is produced from the center of the rosette. The inflorescence may be long with flowers held far away from the plant, or short with flowers nestled in the rosette. It may produce a single flower or many individual flowers and may have colorful leaf-like appendages called scape bracts that serve to attract pollinators and delight bromeliad enthusiasts. With rare exceptions, bromeliads only flower a single time. Once the plant stops producing leaves and starts flowering, it will not make leaves again, but produces new plantlets called "offsets" or "pups." The pups feed off the mother plant until they are large enough to set roots of their own and survive as a separate plant. ❧

Cacti and Succulents

The cactus epitomizes both the ingenuity and paradox of nature. Thick skins and fiendish spines protect cacti from predators, while brilliant flowers lure bees and other pollinators for reproduction. According to John Smolik, an avid fan of cacti and succulents, all cacti bloom. But few people see them because many cactus flowers don't open until nearly midnight and close as soon as the sun starts to rise.

Despite their mystery, John says there is nothing mysterious about growing cacti. "Just don't water too much," he warns. John says he waters his plants every couple of months. ❧

The pad, fruit and bud of a spineless prickly pear

A large agave is surrounded by tangerine bulbine.

Night-blooming cereus cacti

Tropical Fruit

The luscious flavor of freshly picked fruit is one of the sweet rewards enjoyed by Coastal Bend gardeners John Maguire and Lowell Thomas. John always liked citrus fruit, so when he moved to Corpus Christi from Illinois he filled his backyard with tangerine, orange and grapefruit trees. When Lowell and his wife Betty moved to the area from Oklahoma, they were delighted to be able to grow tropical fruit like papaya, avocado, and mango.

Neither John nor Lowell uses pesticides on their gardens. Both have learned through experience that spraying for pests kills beneficial insects and can harm other plants and animals as wells. ❧

John Maguire's citrus trees produce an abundance of sweet oranges (above). Lowell Thomas's papaya trees are heavy laden (right).

Plumeria

Plumeria is a tropical favorite found in many Coastal Bend gardens. Known as the Hawaiian lei flower, the plumeria is actually native to the Carribean and not the Pacific islands, says Jan Shannon.

She says her first plumeria came from a friend in the Rose Society who gave her two sticks and told her to put them in the ground. Being from Nebraska and unfamiliar with plumeria, Jan was not sure what to expect. But, she stuck the two sticks in the ground and soon was surprised by a fragrant, flowering tropical plant. Today, Jan and her husband and fellow gardener, Ron, have more than fifteen varieties of plumeria in their yard. ❧

A collection of fragrant plumerias can transform a lackluster backyard into a tropical escape reminiscent of an island vacation.

Art and culture have influenced gardens and landscaping for centuries. In the Coastal Bend, each new group of immigrants has brought plants, art, and culture from their native land. Today, trimmed hedges and expanses of neatly edged lawns mimic formal gardens of western Europe. Saltillo tile patios and courtyard gardens hidden behind high stucco walls reflect the strong influences of Mexico. Other gardens display creative blends of multiple cultures, or simply an expression of the gardener's own imagination.

Sculpture Garden

Maxine Delano claims her stunning sculpture garden was not the result of conscious planning. Rather, it stems from her love of antiques of all kinds. "I never think consciously where I'll put things. I just buy what I like and figure out where it should go later."

Arches, columns, and statuary are just a sampling of the elaborate yard art in the Delano's backyard. There is even a working chandelier hanging from a tree near the pool. Maxine works with a local brick mason to design and construct many of her garden projects.

Many of her antique pieces have come from her favorite dealer in Angleton, Texas. She makes frequent excursions there to see what treasures he collected on his latest trip to Europe.

"I don't think I ever visit his store without bringing something back," she says.

Maxine also has found a number of interesting pieces locally, such as the intricately designed iron gate that decorates one wall. She says many of her pieces have deteriorated because of age, but that is also part of their interest. She enjoys the stories behind them.

Each sculpture or architectural piece in Maxine's garden creates a dramatic focal point for plantings, and lends an elegant, European charm to the garden. Her flowerbeds are filled with blooming plants. "I like to keep the area along the back fence looking nice for the golfers," she says. ❧

Architectural grouping incorporates a pair of twisted columns that came from Maxine Delano's elementary school near Baytown.

Madagascar palm

Contemporary Garden

The home of Brenda and William Parrish is comprised of four contemporary structures which reflect Mexican influences with a Zen-Contemporary approach. They have used color, texture, natural lighting, and landscaping to create a striking garden that is modern in design yet reflective of ancient traditions. It brings together the best of old and new, east and west, native and exotic.

In designing the garden, the Parrishes wanted the landscape to blend with the colorful stucco exteriors of their home. The original plan was created by Hector J. Villarreal, local landscape designer and owner of Southern Landscapes. Brenda is a Master Gardener and was pleased with everything he drafted.

Water-wise plants such as windmill palms, pecan trees, Chinese fan palms, giant liriope, and blue plumbago were incorporated into the design. Seventy cardboard palms were brought in from Florida. Strangely shaped succulents, such as a Madagascar palm, contrast with the colorful textured walls of the house.

Many of the plants in the Parrish's garden are self-propagating, because Brenda loves giving plants to neighbors and friends. ❧

Lily of the Nile

Mexican Courtyards

Mexican culture is indelibly imprinted on the fabric of South Texas life. Centuries of Spanish influence have colored regional food, clothing, language and architecture as well as names of places and plants.

In designing their custom home, B.J. and Mike Kershaw drew upon traditional Mexican architecture and built a red-tiled, stucco hacienda surrounding a large central courtyard.

The Kershaws' courtyard garden blends their living quarters and garden into a single unit. For B.J. who prefers plants in pots rather than beds, the courtyard is the perfect spot for her many plants. Mike appreciates not having to spend his free time mowing grass.

The Kershaws use a drip irrigation system on a timer to keep the plants watered. B.J. says it makes better use of the water. In the front yard, the Kershaws have used creative planters to add color and interest. ❧

A candelabra cactus (right)
and a red bird plant (far right)
cast interesting shapes on a stucco wall.
The red bird plant is also known
as "Jacob's ladder."

Mexican influences are frequently seen in
gardens and architecture of the Coastal Bend.
At one home, a colorful tiled fountain is the
focal point of an indoor atrium.

Tex-Asian Garden

Faced with poor drainage and limited space, Dixie Oshman combined South Texas Xeriscaping principles and plants with Asian garden design to create her own Tex-Asian style.

In keeping with Asian traditions, Dixie selected and placed rocks with as much care as other gardeners do plants. Rocks play a significant role in Asian landscaping, symbolizing stability and permanence. Zen priests believe the rocks should look as if they naturally came to rest where they lay.

Water is another important element of an oriental garden, representing cleansing and renewal. Dixie's retreat features copper fountains of her own design and a small reflective pool. The sound of trickling water blends with clear, melodic tones of wind chimes, soothing the soul.

In Zen gardens, contrast reflects the variety and vicissitudes of life. In selecting her plants, Dixie looked for varied shapes and textures, as well as the ability to survive the hot, dry climate.

She also combined elements of a Japanese tea garden with a typical Texas-style deck as part of her Tex-Asian design. The covered shelter with teak benches provides an inviting spot where Dixie enjoys sipping coffee and spending a few moments in quiet reflection. ❧

Fountains and a mirror pool carved into a stone add interest to Dixie Oshman's backyard retreat.

An artistically shaped bonsai completes an intriguing garden composition.

The Art of Bonsai

Bonsai is the art of cultivating miniature trees, and it is one of the most widely recognized Asian gardening techniques. Successful bonsai gardeners must possess an artistic sense of form and balance as well as a practical knowledge of growing plants.

In Gail and Gerry Thompson's garden, bonsai trees are strategically displayed, reflecting the beauty of nature in a miniature form. Gail says that they always have liked the peacefulness and low maintenance of an oriental-style garden and had a few bonsais. But, it was a chance encounter with bonsai enthusiast Yvonne Padilla that inspired them to grow bonsais in earnest.

The Thompsons consider Yvonne their mentor. She began growing bonsais more than twenty five years ago and has nearly eighty bonsai plants in her yard, including many Texas natives, several tropicals and some conifers.

"The greatest misconception about bonsais is that because they are small and cute they are houseplants. Bonsais are real trees and shrubs, and require the same outdoor sun and air circulation as their larger brothers and sisters," she says.

Kingman ficus

Pink Pixie bougainvillea

Yvonne Padilla's Brazilian raintree has received statewide recognition from other bonsai growers.

Bonsais can be brought inside for a day or two to use as table decoration, but they need to be kept outside if they are to thrive. Many bonsai gardeners rotate their plants so they can enjoy them both inside and out.

To grow a bonsai, a gardener may start with a seed, a cutting, or dig up a small native plant. In digging for natives, the trick is to look for nice fiber roots and a good shape for the trunk. The plants are collected in pre-bonsai growing containers and kept there for two to four years as they start developing branches. Gardeners use aluminum wire to position and hold developing branches to desired shapes. Once the basic shape of the tree is formed, it is transferred to a bonsai container.

A bonsai container is a small, shallow container that is proportionately balanced to the tree. Balance and proportion are two fundamental concepts in shaping a bonsai. After the tree is transferred to its bonsai container, the gardener will clip the branches and branchlets to cause more twigging and create more depth in the tree's shape. The tree will remain in the same pot for one to five years, over which time the gardener continues to carefully prune and shape the tree. Once the roots outgrow the container, the bonsai is repotted into another bonsai container which is in balance with the overall size and shape of the tree. As part of the repotting process, roots are pruned to keep the tree small.

Yvonne has some bonsai trees that are only five inches tall with half-inch diameter trunks. Others are thirty inches tall with four-inch diameter trunks. She says there are five basic styles of bonsai, upon which another forty styles are based. ❧

Yard Art

Drivers often slow down for a second look at Robert and Lydia Garcia's neatly tended garden where both creativity and plants flourish.

When they first moved into their home nearly forty years ago, the house was on the outskirts of Corpus Christi and surrounded by tall Johnson grass. Little by little, they did what they could to transform the empty lot into a garden full of plants and fascinating yard art.

"It didn't happen overnight," says Robert. But whenever he had an idea for a project, he worked on it until it was finished. Robert and Lydia did all of the work themselves. He taught himself plumbing, carpentry and gardening by looking, watching, and asking questions.

The Garcias are no longer adding or making changes to their garden. But they still decorate their yard for each holiday so that others might enjoy.

Robert and Lydia Garcia used creativity and self-taught skills to transform their yard into a collection of interesting yard art.

Nancy Douglas is another creative gardener whose green thumb and artistic eye have resulted in a yard that makes people stop and take notice. Nancy has gardened all of her life, off and on. After she retired, it became her full-time avocation. "It wasn't supposed to happen, but it took over my life," she says. "I was cursed with a green body, not just a green thumb!"

Nancy has a knack for transforming found objects into intriguing focal points for plantings. She began with cobalt blue bottles she picked up while strolling along the beach. Later she filled her grandchildren's castoff wagons and dump trucks with flowers, as reminders of their younger years, and added them to her garden. ❧

Antique electrical insulators, an old chair and colorful birdhouses are creative additions to Nancy Douglas's garden.

CORPUS CHRISTI BOTANICAL GARDENS & NATURE CENTER

Creating a botanical garden takes time: time for planning, time for planting, time for growing. The Corpus Christi Botanical Society, Inc. was formed in 1983 as a vision to preserve, display and interpret native and adapted flora and fauna of South Texas. The vision became reality when a preliminary Corpus Christi Botanical Gardens opened at its original 110-acre site in 1987. Ten years later in early 1996, the Botanical Gardens moved to its permanent site on 180 acres of uplands, pristine habitat and natural wetlands along Oso Creek.

Over the years, the scope of the Corpus Christi Botanical Gardens has expanded dramatically. In 1999, the non-profit Corpus Christi Botanical Society changed its name to the Botanical and Nature Institute of South Texas, Inc. to better define its educational mission. In 2003, the Botanical Gardens became the Corpus Christi Botanical Gardens & Nature Center to better reflect its commitment to native vegetation and fauna, and emphasize its link to nature tourism.

Urn fountain adorns bed in front of Botanical Gardens & Nature Center Visitor Center.

Today, this excellent venue for youth and adult horticultural and environmental education lets visitors experience the beauty and diversity of South Texas's flora and fauna. The Botanical Gardens & Nature Center features plants displayed in gardens, landscape settings, greenhouses, wetlands, and native areas. Visitors can view exhibits of exotic and adapted plants commonly found in the Coastal Bend, and learn how to include them in their personal yards and gardens. Additionally, a full calendar of gardening and ecology seminars, workshops, and special events brings area residents a multitude of enjoyable eco-education and conservation opportunities.

You'll Love Every Bloomin' Thing!

Hibiscus Garden

The tropical or Chinese hibiscus (*Hibiscus rosa-sinensis*), Corpus Christi's city flower, is showcased in the colorful Hibiscus Garden. The garden features the standard single red 'Brilliant' hibiscus, as well as many other single and double varieties which thrive in local landscapes. Other members of the mallow family are tucked underneath towering fan palms and elegant mesquite trees.

Exhibit House

Within its four-winged lathe structure, the Exhibit House features a myriad of tropical collections including bromeliads, cycads, cacti, and succulents—all of which grow in the Coastal Bend's mix of sub-tropical, and semi-arid climates. While admiring vegetation, visitors can relax on benches near a water feature in the picturesque central courtyard.

Orchid House

The Don Larkin Memorial Orchid Greenhouse, a cornerstone at the Gardens & Nature Center, houses nearly 3,000 orchids, one of the largest collections in the southwestern United States. The climate is controlled by fans, heaters, and a wet-wall. The Orchid House utilizes rainwater collection and reverse osmosis systems to maintain an adequate supply of purified water. Orchid Curator Sam Jones, assisted by members of the South Texas Orchid Society, care for the collection, which has been featured in *Texas Highways* magazine.

Rose Garden & Pavilion

The 35,000 square-foot Rose Garden with its stately roofed pavilion, bricked pathway, and striking Mexican cantera stone fountain is a landmark exhibit of the Botanical Gardens & Nature Center. The Rose Garden's three hundred roses are curated and maintained by the Corpus Christi Rose Society and include hybrid tea roses, floribundas, and miniature roses best suited for the high humidity and heat of the Coastal Bend. Each year the Rose Society tests introductions of new rose varieties in the garden to assess their suitability for local gardens.

Sensory Garden

The Sensory Garden is designed so visitors can experience landscape, and artscape with all of their senses – sight, smell, sound, touch, and taste. In addition to colorful blooms, fragrant herbs, and textured leaves, the Sensory Garden features artscape by local artist Danny O'Dowdy. Limestone couches with tiled serapes delight the eye and intrigue the fingertips. Nearby, visitors' ears are treated to the creak of a windmill and splash of a water pump where two sculpted ranch hands have paused to take a drink.

Sensory Garden artscape includes a windmill and a limestone and ceramic tile "sofa."

Plumeria Collection

Encircling the Exhibit House are more than one hundred varieties of plumeria, one of the largest public outdoor displays in the continental United States. During winter months, the plants are pruned, stripped of leaves, and greenhoused dormant to protect them from possible freezes. The Plumeria Society of South Texas donated, installed, and curates the exhibit.

Hummingbird Garden

During spring and fall migration seasons, the Hummingbird Garden is an excellent spot for viewing these tiny feathered jewels, and learning which colorful plants and vines attract them. The quaint picket-fenced garden is full of vibrant red, orange, purple, and pink blooming perennials easily adapted to home landscapes.

Arid Garden

The large Arid Garden offers visitors an opportunity to admire numerous sizeable species of drought tolerant plants including cacti, succulents and other arid and semi-arid plants in a desert-like setting. The winding path through the rocked exhibit brings visitors to a stairway through mesquite brush leading to the large wetland.

Take a Walk on the Wild Side!

Bird & Butterfly Nature Trail

The shaded Bird & Butterfly Trail provides a pleasant stroll through identified native habitat with numerous birding opportunities. The Birding Tower offers an elevated vantage point for viewing roseate spoonbills, white pelicans, egrets and other coastal birds often seen on Gator Lake. The trail was widened and resurfaced in 2000 to provide handicapped access. The Gardens & Nature Center is a Great Texas Coastal Birding Trail site.

Gator Lake & the Large Wetland

Visitors can learn about coastal wetlands at the Palapa Grande on Gator Lake and the Wetland Awareness Boardwalk, which features creative interpretative signage about wetland plant and animal life and wonderful views of the scenic large wetland area. Wildlife enthusiasts enjoy following tracks of deer, fox, javalina, bobcat and occasionally alligators on the Oso Creek Loop Trail at this Texas Watchable Wildlife site. The Natural Resources Conservation Service, an agency of the United States Department of Agriculture, recognized the Gardens & Nature Center's wetland restoration and improvement project in 2005 for its contribution to environmental conservation and education. ❧

Gator Lake (right) with educational signage; Palapa Grande (below); and Wetlands Awareness Boardwalk after heavy rain (below right).

THE CHRISTMAS MIRACLE

Although most people think of fields covered with white cotton bolls as the closest thing we get to snow in South Texas, Old Man Winter decided that Corpus Christi needed a little of the real stuff in 2004. Not only was Christmas 2004 marked by the largest snowfall on record in Corpus Christi, (officially 4.4 inches) but it was the first White Christmas since 1918! Common sights sometimes taken for granted became extraordinary works of art in the purity of new fallen Christmas snow. Our semi-tropical landscape with palm trees, agave and cacti took on a whole new look with a coating of snow. Corpus Christi Botanical Gardens & Nature Center also was transformed into a winter wonderland. The Gardens & Nature Center were closed on Christmas Day, but luckily, a few adventurous volunteers captured the Christmas miracle in the Gardens on film so we all could enjoy it for years to come. ❧

In Appreciation

Corpus Christi Botanical Gardens & Nature Center
extends its deep appreciation to the individuals and organizations that made this publication possible.

Garden Clubs & Plant Societies
for their garden nominations

Aransas/San Patricio Master Gardeners

Bay Area Garden Guild

Cenizo Garden Club, Mathis

Coastal Bend Cactus and Succulent Society

Corpus Christi African Violet Society

Corpus Christi Area Garden Council, Inc.

Corpus Christi Bonsai Club

Corpus Christi Bromeliad Society

Corpus Christi Garden Club

Corpus Christi Rose Society

Driftwood Garden Club

Hibiscus Garden Club, Aransas Pass

Ingleside Garden Club

Key Allegro Garden Club, Rockport

Kingsville Bird and Wildlife Club

Kingsville Garden Club

Native Plant Society

Nueces County Master Gardeners

Ocean Drive Garden Club

Paisano Garden Club

Palm Society of South Texas

Plumeria Society of South Texas

Port Aransas Garden Club

Portland Garden Club

Retama Garden Club, Alice

Rockport Home and Garden Club

Sinton Garden Club

South Texas Orchid Society

Photographers
for their time and talents

Carmen Bueno, *10 left*

MaryJane Crull, *112 right, 115*

Meredith Dawson, *63 bottom right*

Sam Jones, *117*

Barbra Riley, *93 right*

Nancy Roberts, *2 right, 23 right, 74 right, 79 left*

Jan Shannon, *52 right, 84, 85, 97 left*

Greg Spalding, *8*

Martell Speigner, *114, 116*

John Watson, *all photos not otherwise credited*

AEP is honored to play a supporting role in this project. Page after beautifully illustrated page proves what many of us have known all along: South Texas is one of the true garden spots.

In Appreciation

Corpus Christi Botanical Gardens & Nature Center
also appreciates this opportunity to thank those who have so generously given since the site opened in 1996.

Major Donors

AEP Texas
Anonymous donor
American Bank
Nelwyn Anderson
W.G. "Bill" Bates Memorial Fund
W.L. Bates Company
Behmann Brothers Foundation
Berry Contracting, Inc.
Marshall Boykin, III
Bowen Enterprises, Ltd.
Henry Brennecke
Carlisle Insurance
Citgo Refinery
Coastal Bend Bays & Estuaries Program, Inc.
Coastal Bend Community Foundation
Coastal Management Program/
   Texas General Land Office
Corpus Christi Area Garden Council, Inc.
The late Don and Chauncey Cox
Creveling Dodge

Devary Durrill Foundation
Flint Hills Resources
Frost Bank
Sam Hausman Foods
H-E-B
Steve and June Herbst
John G. and Marie Stella Kenedy
   Memorial Foundation
Amy Shelton McNutt Charitable Trust
Plumeria Society of South Texas
Ed Rachal Foundation
Earl C. Sams Foundation
San Jacinto Title Services
Stanley Smith Horticultural Trust
Blair and Sandy Sterba-Boatwright
Texas Commercial Energy
Texas Forest Service
Texas Parks & Wildlife
Valero Refinery
Whataburger, Inc.

Corpus Christi Botanical Gardens & Nature Center
Executive Committee

Marshall Boykin, III
Judy Creveling
June Herbst
Eric Hamon
John Miller
George Olivarri
Jan Shannon
Cathy Skurow
John Watson
Betty Whitt
Michael Womack

Corpus Christi Botanical Gardens & Nature Center
Staff

MaryJane Crull
Debe Holt
John Parish
Paul Thornton

INDEX OF GARDENS

Numbers in italics refer to page numbers and locations

Larry and Donna Frederick's *La Casita* patio